Peak District: **Mysterious Walks**

Text: *David Dunford*
Series editor: *Tony Bowerman*
Photographs: *David Dunford, Dennis Kelsall, Jonathan Clitheroe (cc-by-sa/2.0), Colin Park (cc-by-sa/2.0), Adobe Stock, Shutterstock, Dreamstime, Unsplash*

Design: *Carl Rogers & Laura Hodgkinson*

© Northern Eye Books Limited 2022

David Dunford has asserted his rights under the Copyright, Designs and Patents Act, 1988 to be identified as the author of this work. All rights reserved.

This book contains mapping data licensed from the Ordnance Survey with the permission of the Controller of Her Majesty's Stationery Office. © Crown copyright 2022 All rights reserved. Licence number 100047867.

ISBN 978-1-914589-12-6

A CIP catalogue record for this book is available from the British Library.

Important Advice: The routes described in this book are undertaken at the reader's own risk. Walkers should take into account their level of fitness, wear suitable footwear and clothing, and carry food and water. It is also advisable to take the relevant OS map with you in case you get lost and leave the area covered by our maps.

Whilst every care has been taken to ensure the accuracy of the route directions, the publishers cannot accept responsibility for errors or omissions, or for changes in the details given. Nor can the publisher and copyright owners accept responsibility for any consequences arising from the use of this book.

If you find any inaccuracies in either the text or maps, please write or email us at the address below. Thank you.

First published in 2022 by
Northern Eye Books Limited
Northern Eye Books, Tattenhall, Cheshire CH3 9PX

tony@northerneyebooks.co.uk

For sales enquiries, please call 01928 723 744

www.northerneyebooks.co.uk

Cover: *Eyam - 'Plague Village' (Walk 3).*

Instagram: @northerneyebooks
Twitter: @Northerneyeboo

Printed in the EU by Latitude on woodland-friendly FSC stock

Contents

The Peak District National Park 4

Top 10 Walks: Mysterious Walks 6

1 | Robin Hood's Picking Rods 8

2 | Robin Hood's Cave 14

3 | Eyam – 'Plague Village' 20

4 | Gardom's and Birchen Edges 26

5 | Solomon's Temple 30

6 | Lud's Church 36

7 | Rowtor Rocks & Cratcliff 40

8 | Thor's Cave 46

9 | Thorpe & Fenny Bentley 52

10 | Halter Devil Chapel 58

Useful Information 64

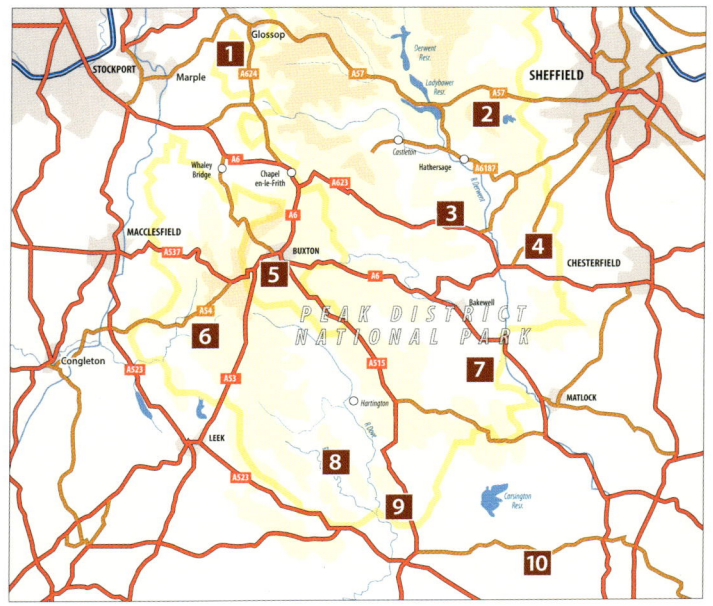

The Peak District National Park

EVEN THE NAME CONCEALS A MYSTERY. Forget the obvious: a visitor expecting towering peaks will be disappointed, as the name comes from the Pecsaetan tribe who once lived here. But there's a twist: the Anglo-Saxon means "settlers of the Pec"…and that word pec has the same root as our peak, the dialect pike and the Pyrenean pic. So, ultimately, the Peak District is named after its peaks, after all.

The Peak District is broadly defined by the conurbations at its corners: Manchester, Sheffield, Derby and Stoke. Within this rectangle, the National Park forms a rough oval of around 550 square miles.

The area is traditionally divided into the Dark Peak — peat moorland edged by gritstone, with rugged villages in the valleys — and the softer White Peak, upland pastures defined by drystone walls, divided by gorges and limestone villages. The eastern and western moors are similar to the Dark Peak, but have their own subtly distinctive characters.

Fog shrouds ancient woodland in Monk's Dale, in the Peak District

Mysteries of the Peak

The Peak District was occupied by humans long before the Pecsaetans and in each era man has left his mark, from prehistoric standing stones and rock art, through the folk legends, crosses and churches of the Middle Ages, to post-medieval follies and puzzling relics of the extraction of lime and lead.

The varied geology of the area throws up natural curiosities too: its dark gritstone has wind-sculpted tors and edges, while its gleaming limestone hides caves and subterranean rivers.

"And now I am come to this wonderful place, the Peak, where you will expect I should do as some others have, (I think, foolishly) done before me, viz. tell you strange long stories of wonders as (I must say) they are most weakly call'd"

– Daniel Defoe

TOP 10 Walks: Mysterious Walks

CURATING CURIOSITIES IN THE PEAK DISTRICT IS CONTAGIOUS: William Camden listed 'wonders three and beauties three' in the High Peak as early as 1586. Thomas Hobbes compiled *The Wonders of the Peak* in 1636 and Charles Cotton, of *Compleat Angler* fame, published his version 50 years later. This contribution to the genre is likewise intended to inspire and inform exploration of the Peak's mysteries. Each walk visits at least one curiosity — and often more — and includes details of a nearby source of refreshment.

Robin Hood's Picking Rods — page 8

Robin Hood's Cave — page 14

Eyam 'Plague Village' — page 20

Gardom's & Birchen Edges — page 26

Solomon's Temple — page 30

Lud's Church — page 36

Cratcliff Hermitage — page 40

Thor's Cave — page 46

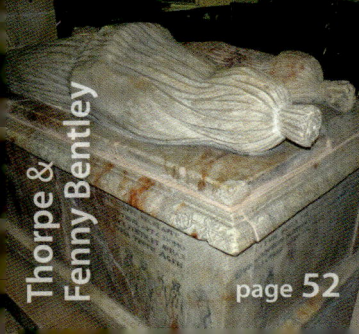

Thorpe & Fenny Bentley — page 52

Halter Devil Chapel — page 58

8 ◆ TOP 10 WALKS **PEAK DISTRICT: Mysterious Walks**

Two time-worn cross shafts make up Robin Hood's Picking Rods

walk 1

Robin Hood's Picking Rods
A 1000-year-old landmark, close to an even older relic

What to expect: *A pretty hamlet, a stream valley and rough grazing land*

Distance/time: 6 kilometres/3¾ miles. Allow 2½ hours

Start: Rowarth car park (free), SK22 1EF

Grid Ref: SK011892

Ordnance Survey map: OL1 The Peak District *(Dark Peak Area)*

After the Walk: The Little Mill Inn, Hollinsmoor Road, Rowarth, High Peak SK22 1EB | www.thelittlemillinn.co.uk | 01663 747678

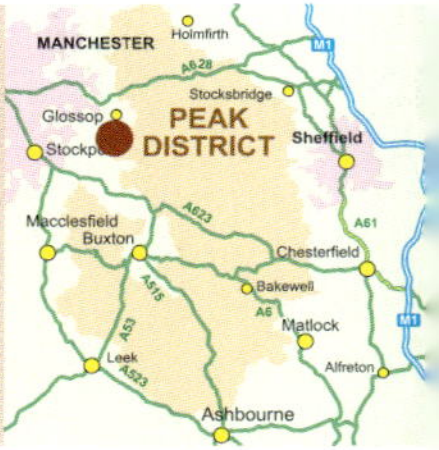

Walk outline
From a pretty gritstone hamlet our route heads up an intimate stream valley, then climbs to the top of a ridge with views to Kinder Scout to the east and Manchester and the Cheshire Plain to the west. Having visited the isolated double cross-shaft of Robin Hood's Picking Rods (and a nearby cup-and-ring-marked rock) we return to Rowarth, via a charming pub in a former millhouse. Wide views abound throughout in this underrated and little-visited corner of the Peak District.

Robin Hood's Picking Rods
In the early Middle Ages, the surrounding land was owned by Basingwerk Abbey, near Holywell in North Wales. The shepherd monks erected wayside crosses to aid travellers and to mark ecclesiastical divisions. Robin Hood's Picking Rods is unusual in combining both, having two cross shafts springing from the same *socle* (the large stone socket). In folklore, they are said to have been used by Robin Hood while stringing his bow. At some point, unknown hands have carved N and S onto the shafts, perhaps as an aid to navigation.

Cup-and-ring-marks

Bilberries

The Walk

1. From the public **car park** in **Goddards Lane**, turn right and walk into **Rowarth** village, where two terraces of cottages overlook a village green. Turn right at **Anderton House** then, just before a traditional K6 telephone booth, turn left onto a footpath which descends by a stream to a **ford**.

2. Cross the track over a stile opposite and continue up the valley with the stream on your right. Pass a **footbridge** and a stile and continue along the stream until you meet a crossing track above a **ford**. Turn left, away from the stream, and follow the track uphill to a gate into a metalled driveway.

3. Turn right and then very shortly left at a footpath sign, and climb a short rocky path to a stile before continuing uphill along the edge of a horse paddock to a junction of paths. Take the path up the slope, signposted to 'Cown Edge'. The path climbs between gorse bushes and the remains of **small quarries** to a stile in a wall, beyond which follow a wall on

© Crown copyright and/or database right. All rights reserved. Licence number 100047867

Walk 1 – **Robin Hood's Picking Rods** ♦ 11

The Little Mill Inn has a replica waterwheel beside the brook

the left, staying left when a more obvious path heads off to the right. Pass (but do not cross) a stile at a fence corner and walk above the buildings of **Near Slack Farm** and its plantation.

4. Beyond the last of the trees, the path continues along a fence to join a fenced track to Far Slack. Continue ahead past above the **farm buildings** to a gate into a track.

5. Turn left and follow the track to **Robin Hood's Picking Rods**. Eighty metres before you reach the obvious pair of shafts, look out for the **cup-and-ring marked rock** (a fairly insignificant boulder less than a metre square) immediately to the right of the track.

6. Continue along the track beyond the Picking Rods. After a little over a quarter of a mile, turn left over a **ladder stile** in the wall. Follow a narrow path across rushy pasture to a stile next to a gate in a fence near a small **pond**. Bear right across the next field to a stone step stile at the end of a wall. The path beyond skirts a **small quarry** then follows the wall to another stile into a track leading out to the road at **Pistol Farm**.

Robin Hood's Picking Rods beside the track high on Cown Edge

7. Turn left and follow the public road downhill for little under quarter of a mile; ignore a signposted footpath on the left, then turn left into a Restricted Byway.

Follow the byway to **Ringstones Farm** (*whose name may indicate a now-lost stone circle*) then continue along the metalled driveway to the right of the farm and out to the public road just below the **Children's Inn**.

8. Turn left and walk down the road towards Rowarth. Continue past the entrance to **Goddards Lane** (unless you require a short-cut omitting the pub) down to the **Little Mill Inn**.

In the late 18th and early 19th century there were five or six watermills strung out along the Rowarth Brook, supporting a school and chapel in the village. The terraced cottages around the village green housed the mill workers, whereas handsome Anderton House, a Grade II listed building dating from 1787, was the residence of a mill owner. Similarly, the house now occupied by the Little Mill Inn was built for another of the mill owners. The remains of the adjacent candlewick mill and its waterwheel were destroyed by floods in the 1930s; the current large-diameter wheel is a modern replica.

9. Just before the pub, take a bridleway on the left next to a house, which follows

Walk 1 – **Robin Hood's Picking Rods** ♦ 13

a concrete driveway to a smallholding, with the stream on your right. Beyond the last house the bridleway continues as a rough path before emerging at the end of a lane in **Rowarth**.

Pass the telephone kiosk and retrace your steps to the car park, turning left at **Anderton House**, to complete the walk. ♦

Prehistoric rock art?

Cup-and-ring-marked rocks are commoner further north, but the Peak District has a few rare examples of this cryptic prehistoric artform. Experts have counted nine golf-ball-sized cup marks on the trackside boulder here; while less impressive than examples elsewhere, this relic proves that this remote area was occupied in the Bronze Age. Like the nearby Robin Hood's Picking Rods, it may have acted as a boundary marker.

The womb-like chamber of Robin Hood's Cave below Stanage Edge

walk 2

Robin Hood's Cave
Echoes of an outlaw partnership below Stanage Edge

What to expect: *Sustained descent and ascent; rocky ground and vertical drops on Stanage Edge*

Distance/time: 7 kilometres/4¼ miles. Allow 3 hours

Start: Free parking at Hook's Carr car park; if full, try Hollin Bank ¾ mile to the northeast

Grid Ref: SK 246 832

Ordnance Survey map: OL1 The Peak District *(Dark Peak Area)*

After the Walk: The Scotsman's Pack, School Lane, Hathersage S32 1BZ | www.scotsmanspackcountryinn.co.uk | 01433 650253

Walk outline
Starting at a high car park below the climber's playground of Stanage Edge, this route descends via moorland to Hathersage church, set within a medieval ringwork. The pubs and cafés of Hathersage are within walking distance.

The return route climbs past historic North Lees Hall to a car park and toilets, then steepens through bouldery woodland to the top of Stanage Edge. The return along the edge is largely level, with views over the Derwent valley. Robin Hood's Cave offers a final highlight before the short descent to the car park.

Stanage Edge
Stanage is a classic destination for rock-climbers. Robin Hood's Cave lies just below the lip of the edge and access requires minor scrambling and a head for heights; the reward is a superb natural balcony in the cliff face. The short cave passage behind the opening is unusual among Peak District caves firstly in occurring in gritstone rather than soluble limestone, and secondly because its eroded curves were mostly formed by wind rather than water.

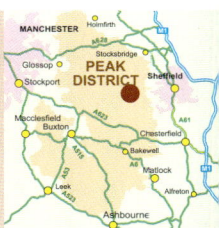

Little John's Grave

Red grouse

The Walk

1. From the roadside **car park**, walk to the adjacent road junction and turn right. Beyond a cattle grid, turn right through a gate onto **Open Access land** and follow the path across the moor, climbing slightly and passing to the left of **Carhead Rocks**. Descend steeply through bracken to a hand-gate into a metalled driveway.

2. Turn right along the driveway, then bear left and downhill past a **stone barn** to **Kimber Court Farm**. Beyond the farm, continue downhill along the track to **Moorseats**, where the stone-setted driveway swings right and left below the house. Follow the driveway across the hillside to **Carr Head** and continue downhill beyond a gate along a metalled lane.

3. After 580 metres, the lane passes through the ramparts of the **Camp Green ringwork** and winds between houses.

Camp Green ringwork was probably built shortly after the Norman Conquest and encloses a circular area with a diameter of about 60m. The surviving defensive embankment

© Crown copyright and/or database right. All rights reserved. Licence number 100047867

Looking down on the gritstone balcony outside Robin Hood's Cave

is still substantial and was enhanced by an outer ditch.

At a road junction, turn right and walk up to **Hathersage Parish Church**. Turn left through the **lychgate** and walk to the left of the church, passing the truncated shaft of the churchyard cross on your right and **Little John's Grave** on your left.

The authenticity of the grave of Little John, Robin Hood's second-in-command, is open to question. If they are to be trusted, measurements of a now-lost thighbone exhumed from the grave in the 18th century would indicate that the deceased was around eight feet tall. Nearby is a medieval cross base, and the church itself has grotesque carvings and a delightful window featuring moorland wildlife.

Continue past the church tower and exit the churchyard to a car park. Turn right past a walled garden, then turn left through a hand-gate.

4. Follow the footpath with the **embankment of the ringwork** on your right, then turn left and descend via steps to a **clapper bridge** over a stream. Ignoring a path off to the left, follow the gappy hedge ahead of you up the slope.

Miles of golden moorland spread out below Stanage Edge

At a waymark post, leave the hedge and bear right to the top right-hand corner of the field. Follow the left-hand hedge beyond a gate to **Cow Close**, above which the path crosses a small stream valley. Descend to cross a track and follow the driveway to the right to a stream, beyond which turn left past a menage to a stile into a road.

5. Cross the road into the driveway to **North Lees Hall** and follow it uphill to the building. Beyond the Hall, turn right before a farm entrance to a gate. Follow the obvious path across the field beyond to a gate into **coniferous woodland**, and continue with a rocky stream below and to your right. As you approach the top of the wood, turn left up rocky steps to a toilet block and exit to the road.

6. Take the path opposite and climb to a gate into woodland (**Stanage Plantation**). Follow the obvious slabbed path through the wood to a gate, then climb the rocky path beyond obliquely up to the top of **Stanage Edge**.

7. Turn right and pick your way along the edge path, passing through a gap between a wall and fence above the plantation. After a little under half a mile, a vague path from **Standedge Pole** (visible to your left) joins the edge path. 200 metres beyond this point, **Robin**

Hood's Cave is accessible via a broad bouldery ledge below the overhanging edge on your right.

8. Continue along the edge path for a further 300 metres beyond the Cave, then (well before the triangulation pillar on a rise ahead) pick your way down through the rocks on your right onto the obvious path leading down the slope to **Hook's Carr car park** to complete the walk. ♦

North Lees Hall

North Lees Hall, built in 1594, is an Elizabethan tower house that provided the inspiration for Thornfield Hall, home of Mr Rochester in Charlotte Brontë's classic novel Jane Eyre. *The Hall was used as a film location in the 2005 version of* Pride and Prejudice *starring Keira Knightley, and also* The Other Boleyn Girl *(2008). Monuments to the real-life Eyre family can be found in the church at Hathersage.*

A skull and crossbones carved on a box tomb in Eyam churchyard

walk 3

Eyam – 'Plague Village'
Echoes of an outlaw partnership below Stanage Edge

What to expect:
A stiff climb and some uneven ground on the hill above the village

Distance/time: 5 kilometres/3¼ miles. Allow 2 hours

Start: Free car park off Hawkhill Road, Eyam (or, if full, pay-and-display opposite museum) S32 5QP

Grid Ref: SK 216 767

Ordnance Survey map: OL24 The Peak District *(White Peak Area)*

After the Walk: The Miners Arms, Water Lane, Eyam S32 5RG | www.theminersarmseyam.co.uk | 01433630853

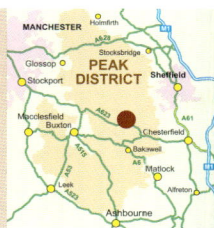

Walk outline
This short route visits most of the visible relics of the plague that claimed the lives of so many of Eyam's inhabitants. We start by climbing the steep edge behind the village to Mompesson's Well, then return via woodland to the village, with opportunities to visit the Riley and Lydgate Graves, the 'plague cottages' and finally Cucklet Church, a spectacular double natural arch where Reverend Mompesson preached during the outbreak.

Stanage Edge
The plague came to Eyam in 1665, probably in a bale of flea-infested cloth delivered from London to a local tailor, whose assistant was the first victim. Led by the rector, William Mompesson, the village elected to self-isolate. Up to half of the villagers perished during the outbreak, which lasted for 14 months. Neighbouring parishioners and landowners left food and other necessities for collection on stones around the village periphery, and at the well now named after the rector.

Cucklet Church

Forget-me-nots

The Walk

1. From the **car park**, turn left down **Hawkhill Road** to the **main street** through the village. Turn right and after 100m pass the end of **Little Edge** and a couple of "**plague cottages**". Just after **Richard Furness' House**, turn right up a driveway between stone cottages, with a wooden fingerpost. Go through a hand-gate into a field; beyond the house to the right of the path is the **grave of Humphrey Merrill**, *the village herbalist, who died in September 1666.*

2. At the top of the field, turn left through a hand-gate before a house, then turn right to cross the driveway and follow the garden wall to a gate. Walk up to the top right-hand corner of the next field, where another gate gives access to the site of **Highcliffe Mine**, a former lead mine.

Beyond the **interpretation panel**, follow the wall on your right then climb steeply through gorse to a gate into woodland. Continue along an old mossy wall then through the trees to cross a small stream to a gate into a meadow. Shortly afterwards, another gate gives access to

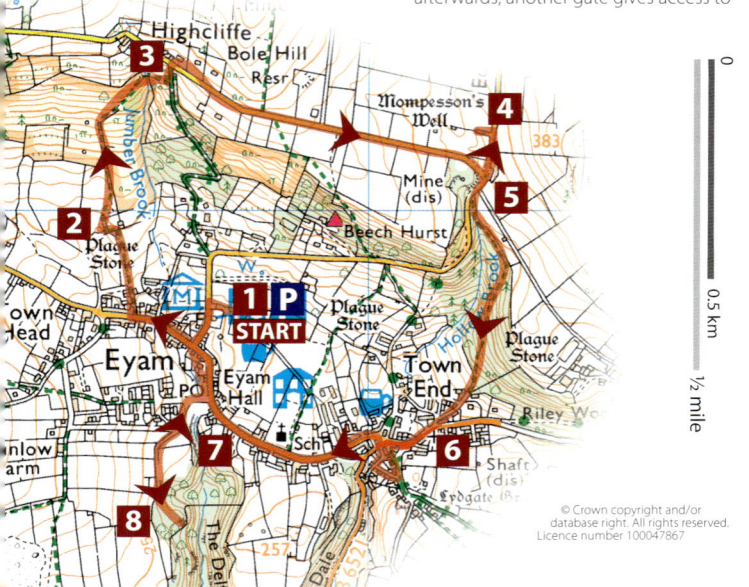

© Crown copyright and/or database right. All rights reserved. Licence number 100047867

The poignant 'Riley family graves' in fields outside Eyam

a rocky byway, where you turn left up to the public road.

3. Turn right and follow the road for half a mile, with views over Eyam and the surrounding countryside. After the entrance to **Ladywash Mine**, below the **chimney** on the left, you reach a T-junction.

4. Turn left to visit **Mompesson's Well** before returning to the junction.

5. Continue past the **Eyam village sign** and a private driveway on the left, then turn left through a squeeze stile (signposted to 'Eyam'). The wooded path leads above a stream valley and under electricity wires, then through a stand of conifers before bearing right and descending steeply back to **Eyam village**.

At the bottom of the path, join the lane down to the **main village street** (a there-and-back diversion to view the **Riley Graves**, not described here, is available via New Road and Riley Lane to the left).

6. Turn right and walk down **The Causeway** to the **square** in the centre of

Eyam Hall is framed by its carved stone gate pillars

the village. By the telephone kiosk, take a left up **The Lydgate** to visit the **Lydgate Graves**.

Beyond the graves, turn immediately right, past some 20th-century housing, and at the end of the lane turn right above a rock face. In front of a pretty pair of whitewashed cottages, turn left. Cross the square to the bus shelter and turn left. Pass the end of **Glebe Park** and continue along to the **church**.

Having visited the church and churchyard, continue along the main street, passing several more 'plague cottages'.

In an attempt to restrict the spread of infection, the dead were buried by their own relatives, close to their homes, as at the Riley and Lydgate Graves. Of the known victims, only Mompesson's wife Catherine is buried in the churchyard, close to the Anglo-Saxon cross.

Visitors to the churchyard also seek out the gravestone of Harry Bagshaw, a cricketer for Derbyshire and the MCC, with its shattered wicket and raised umpire's finger signalling his final dismissal.

7. Just beyond **Eyam Hall**, turn left into **New Close**. Beyond the Hall car park, turn left into **Dunlow Lane**. Pass some houses on the corner, then turn left into a walled track with a fingerpost to

Walk 3 – **Eyam – 'Plague Village'** ♦ 25

Cucklet Church. At the end of the track, turn left via the stile or gate into a field. Walk down the slope, as indicated by another fingerpost, to the **cave** above the woodland edge. It is daylit throughout and fun to explore, though somewhat rocky.

8. Return to **Eyam Hall** by the same route. On regaining the main street, turn left, then after 150 metres turn right into **Hawkhill Road** to return to the start point to complete the walk. ♦

Eyam Cross

This well-preserved Celtic cross dates from the 8th or 9th century and is richly decorated with interlacing scrollwork and Anglo-Saxon Christian imagery. It retains its head, unusually, but has lost a foot or so of its shaft. It was found beside a moorland trackway and moved to the churchyard in the 18th century. Nearby is Catherine Mompesson's 17th-century chest tomb; her ghost is said to haunt the churchyard and pause as she passes the cross.

26 ♦ TOP 10 WALKS **PEAK DISTRICT: Mysterious Walks**

Nelson's Monument, erected on Birchen Edge in 1810

walk 4

Gardom's & Birchen Edges
Rock carvings from prehistory to Trafalgar

What to expect: *Sometimes boggy heathland with rocky sections and a steep descent*

Distance/time: 4 kilometres/2½ miles. Allow 1½ hours

Start: Birchen Edge Pay-and-display car park adjacent to Robin Hood pub at A619/B6050 junction; DE45 1PQ

Grid Ref: SK 280 721

Ordnance Survey map: OL24 The Peak District *(White Peak Area)*

After the Walk: The Robin Hood, Chesterfield Road, Baslow DE45 1PQ | www.robinhoodbaslow.co.uk | 01629700888

Walk outline
This short walk climbs gently to Gardom's Edge, then diverts through birch woodland past a standing stone to a spectacular prehistoric cup-and-ring-marked rock. We then climb to the trig point on Birchen Edge, from where it's a short stroll along the edge to Nelson's Monument, the Three Ships rocks and the descent back to the start.

Stanage Edge
The standing stone on Gardom's Edge is around 1.5 metres tall and has been interpreted as an astronomical marker. It has been carefully aligned by packing stones beneath the surface, so that its leaning edge would have been illuminated by the Neolithic midsummer sun. Nearby is the replica cup-and-ring-marked rock (see page 29).

Nelson's Monument on Birchen Edge was erected in 1810, five years after the admiral died at Trafalgar. Three prominent gritstone outcrops nearby are carved with the names of ships from his battle fleet.

Standing stone

Ring ouzel

The Walk

1. From the **National Trust car park**, walk through the car park of the **Robin Hood pub** and out to the **A619**. Turn right along the pavement and pass **Robin Hood Farm** and a campsite entrance.

2. A hundred metres on, turn right over a **stone step stile** and through a gate. Follow the obvious path gently uphill through boulder-strewn grass and bracken until you pass a large outcrop on the right (the **Cat Stone**).

3. Go through a gateway and, leaving the obvious path, turn right to follow the wall, which curves left to another gateway, beyond which is a line of three cairns known as the **Three Men**, built in the 19th century on top of a prehistoric funereal site. Continue roughly parallel to the wall with **Gardom's Edge** on your left.

4. After about 500 metres, divert round a short projecting spur of drystone wall. Hidden in the corner behind it is a gate leading into the **birch woodland** on your right. A narrow path leads to a leaning **standing stone**. Ignoring the obvious path across the open land ahead of you, follow an indistinct path to the right, staying within the trees, which leads to the **cup-and-ring-marked rock**. Continue beyond the carved rock in the same direction, alongside a low line of boulders, part of a Neolithic enclosure known as **Meg's Walls**.

5. When you meet a modern drystone wall, turn left and follow it towards Birchen Edge. After 450 metres you reach the corner of the wall, at the end of the enclosed fields

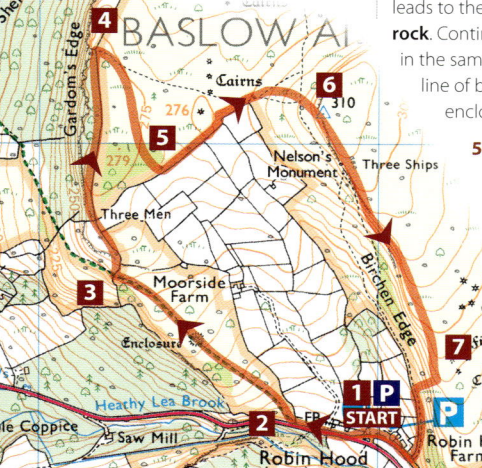

© Crown copyright and/or database right. All rights reserved. Licence number 100047867

The 'Three Ships' rocks and Nelson's Monument on Birchen Edge

on your right. Carry straight on through heather and bracken to a **prominent boulder**. Cross another path and bear half-right up a rocky path to the trig point at the top of **Birchen Edge**.

6. Turn right to **Nelson's Monument** and the **Three Ships**. Beyond the monument, continue along the declining edge until you reach an inspection cover.

7. Turn right here and pick your way down the steep slope. When you meet the path at the bottom of the slope, turn left and follow it back to the **B6050** road. Turn right to return to the car park, to complete the walk. ♦

Prehistoric art?
Gardom's Edge cup-and-ring-marked rock was only uncovered in the 1960s, but subsequent weathering led to a decision to protect it by burying it beneath a replica cast in fibreglass resin. Although larger examples of cup-and-ring-marked rocks are to be found further north, this is by far the best example in the Peak District. Their exact purpose remains a mystery.

30 ◆ TOP 10 WALKS **PEAK DISTRICT: Mysterious Walks**

Solomon's Temple is a Victorian folly on Grin Low hill, near Buxton

walk 5

Solomon's Temple

A walk shaped by limestone: caves, kilns and an industrial/geological freak

What to expect:
Gradual climb through woodland with rocky ground, rough pasture and some road walking

Distance/time: 5.5 kilometres/3½ miles. Allow 2 hours

Start: Poole's Cavern car park (pay and display), SK17 9DQ

Grid Ref: SK 050 725

Ordnance Survey map: OL24 The Peak District *(White Peak Area)*

After the Walk: The Old Sun, 33 High Street, Buxton SK17 6HA | www.theoldsuninnbuxton.co.uk | 01298937986

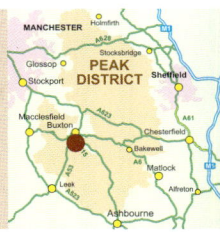

Walk outline

From Poole's Cavern, a commercial show cave, this route climbs through the deciduous woodland of Grin Low and Buxton Country Park, then crosses flower-rich grassland with limestone outcrops to Solomon's Tower, a listed folly and fine viewpoint. After a steep descent and some road walking, we pass a surprising and little-known calcium curiosity then return via sheep pastures quartered by Ravens. The interested can seek out a swallet where a stream disappears into a limestone pothole.

Calcite formations

Grin Low & Stanley Moor

Lime has been extracted around Buxton since the 17th century. The 6th Duke of Devonshire planted the woods on Grin Low and commissioned the building of Solomon's Temple to provide work for unemployed lime workers. On Stanley Moor, streams running off the Axe Edge gritstone reach permeable limestone and sink into swallets, notably Plunge Hole. This water has been dye-traced to the Wye Head resurgence, below Poole's Cavern. Sadly, the potential for significant cave passages is thought to be limited.

Raven

A stream disappearing into Plunge Hole – a 'swallet'

The Walk

1. At the rear of the car park next to **Poole's Cavern**, climb a flight of steps with wooden railings to a path junction. Ignoring the stepped path ahead, turn left here, signposted to 'Solomon's Temple', and follow the yellow-waymarked route, keeping right at a fork. The path ascends gradually through the woods, passing a **wooden carving of a seated lime-worker** next to the remains of a **limekiln**.

2. As you near the top of the trees, keep right at another path junction to a stile leading into open grassland. Bear left through more **old lime workings** and follow the path up to **Solomon's Temple** at the highest point. *A stone staircase inside the tower gives access to an upper floor with views over Buxton.*

3. From the tower, drop off to the right (south) through a low **limestone outcrop** to cross a stile in a wall. Follow the path ahead, which leads downhill, winding through further small outcrops to a second stile in a fence. Cross the final field to a stile next to a gate onto **Grin Low Road**.

Walk 5 – **Solomon's Temple** ♦ 33

4. Turn left and follow the road downhill with views ahead to Harpur Hill, overlooked by a hilltop tumulus known as **Fox Low**. *In the valley on your right, notice how the stream has cut a deep gash through the friable lime spoil.*

5. At the bottom of the hill, leave the road into a farm track on the right and cross a stile by a gate and then a **bridge** over a side-stream. The track leaves the stream and zig-zags up the valley side; the footpath takes a short cut across the first bend to join the track further up alongside a wall, with views up the valley of the leachate plume.

From the 1830s to the 1950s calcium-rich spoil was tipped into this valley below the limeworks of Harpur Hill. The subsequent action of groundwater and the culverted stream has formed a peculiar feature known as a 'leachate plume', whereby the entire valley floor has become covered in terraces and dams of whitish calcium carbonate.

6. Follow the track uphill along the wall then, when it swings right, follow another short-cut on the left steeply up to **Countess Cliff Farm**. Rather than going through the gate into the farmyard, follow a path through a hand-gate

© Crown copyright and/or database right. All rights reserved. Licence number 100047867

34 ♦ TOP 10 WALKS **PEAK DISTRICT: Mysterious Walks**

Solomon's Temple, or Grinlow Tower, overlooking Buxton

on the right and up concrete steps to skirt to the right of the farm.

7. Beyond the **farm buildings**, descend steps to a farm track and bear right, ignoring a stile into fields on the left. Follow the track across open fields with views to Axe Edge (ahead) and Grin Low (right). After a gate, the track curves right then left and descends to a wooded area below the breached embankment of the disused **Stanley Moor Reservoir**.

8. Follow the track round to the right, crossing the **reservoir outflow**. At the end of the trees, the track strikes out across rough pasture in the direction of Grin Low. At the bottom of an obvious **shakehole** on the left, a small stream trickles through lodged boulders into a swallet, known as **Plunge Hole**. Returning to the main track, follow it across **Stanley Moor**, ignoring a grassy track heading obliquely off to the left.

9. Beyond a gate, a driveway leads out to the public road. Cross and follow the road opposite into **Grin Low and Buxton Country Park**. Pass a cattle grid and follow the road uphill to a bench. Here, turn left across the grassy hilltop and pass to the left of a deep **disused quarry**.

10. Descend to a wooden hand-gate

Walk 5 – **Solomon's Temple** ♦ 35

and go down steps into the woods. Follow the blue-waymarked path ahead, which winds through the woods with intermittent steps before descending more consistently down towards **Poole's Cavern**. At the foot of a flight of steps, cross the path you set out on earlier and descend the final steps to the car park to complete the walk. ♦

Underground wonders
Poole's Cavern is well known for its 'poached egg' stalagmites, whose relatively rapid formation was hastened by lime working on the hillsides above and whose colours are caused by iron and organic impurities in the calcium-rich waters. In 1998, ground-penetrating radar identified an extension of the cave which, tantalisingly, has been viewed via remote cameras lowered into a borehole but has not yet been breached by humans.

Lud's Church is a deep, hidden rocky cleft above the River Dane

walk 6

Lud's Church

A legendary location deep in the woods above the charming Dane valley

What to expect:
Woodland walking, uneven underfoot, and a dramatic rocky cleft

Distance/time: 5 kilometres/3 miles. Allow 2 hours

Start: Gradbach car park near Flash SK17 0SU. May be busy at peak times. Additional parking is sometimes provided (for a fee) at nearby farms

Grid Ref: SJ 998 662

Ordnance Survey map: OL24 The Peak District *(White Peak Area)*

After the Walk: Gradbach Mill Café | 01260 227000 | www.gradbach.co.uk/riverside-cafe

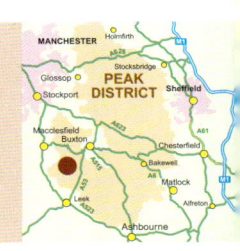

Walk outline

From Gradbach Mill on the stripling Dane, our route crosses Black Brook and then climbs steeply through bird-filled woodlands to the Millstone Grit outcrop of Castle Rock. We then enter the deep rocky cleft of Lud's Church, through which the path passes excitingly before exiting via a rocky staircase. More woodland walking follows before the descent to Black Brook.

Lud's Church

An overhanging rock resembling a face in the cliffs of Lud's Church is identified as the Green Knight, Sir Gawain's opponent in a 14th-century chivalric poem. Dialect words within the work suggest that the unknown author came from this area, and Lud's Church may be the 'Green Chapel' of the tale (*though see also Walk 8 for another candidate*). A congregation of Lollards is thought to have worshipped in secret in the chasm in the 15th century and the capture of Walter de Ludbank, an adherent of the persecuted sect, here may have inspired its name.

Rustic stone sign

Green hairstreak butterfly

The Walk

1. From the **car park**, turn right along the lane, with the river on your right. Climb past the entrance to **Greensytch Farm** then turn right at the gates to **Gradbach Mill** and walk down the drive to the former **youth hostel**. Bear right then left in front of the main building onto a signposted public footpath alongside the **river**. Leave the river up some stone steps into a field and pass behind the café before turning right into a hedged path. Turn left and follow the path for 300 metres to squeeze stile and bear right to descend to **Black Brook**.

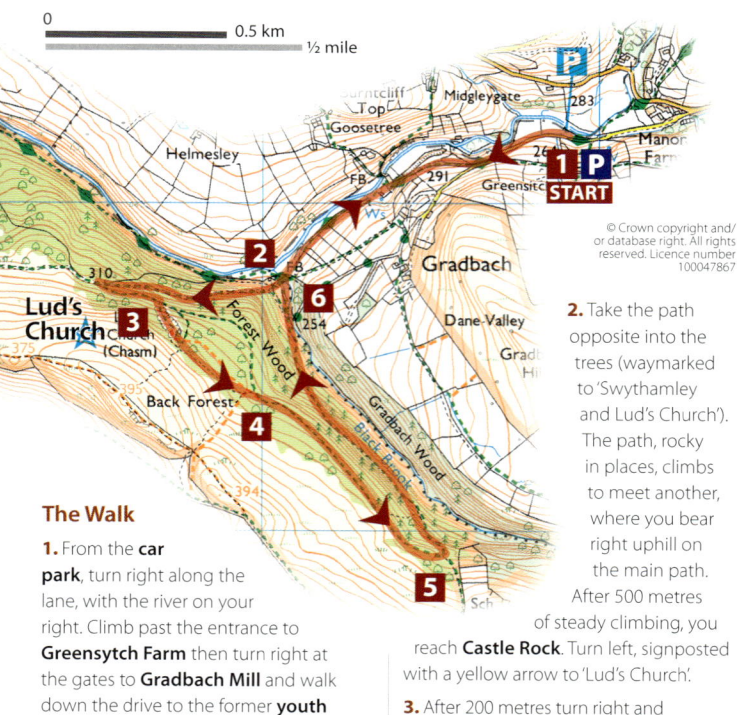

2. Take the path opposite into the trees (waymarked to 'Swythamley and Lud's Church'). The path, rocky in places, climbs to meet another, where you bear right uphill on the main path. After 500 metres of steady climbing, you reach **Castle Rock**. Turn left, signposted with a yellow arrow to 'Lud's Church'.

3. After 200 metres turn right and descend carefully into **Lud's Church**, which is often muddy. At the far end, keep right at a junction (turn round to spot the Green Knight) and exit the ravine via a flight of rough steps on the right. Turn left, with the tail of the ravine on your left, then follow the footpath ahead over boardwalks through birch woodland.

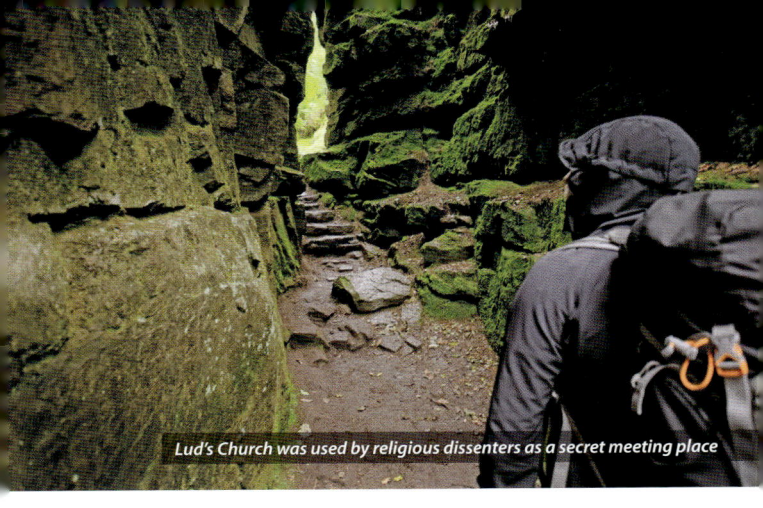

Lud's Church was used by religious dissenters as a secret meeting place

4. At a junction beyond the boardwalks, 250m from Lud's Church, go straight on (signposted 'Gradbach/Roaches'). Another junction quickly follows; turn right ('Roaches'). This path winds along the top of the wood for 750 metres before dropping slightly to meet another path below beech trees.

5. Turn left ('Gradbach and Danebridge') and follow a root-strewn path downhill, steeply at first, with the valley of **Black Brook** to your right. Eventually the path descends to the stream. Pass a **ford** and continue alongside the brook to the **footbridge** you crossed earlier.

6. Cross the stream and retrace your earlier steps back to the car park via Gradbach Mill to complete the walk. ♦

Roaches Grit

Lud's Church is thought to be post-glacial: in geological terms fairly recent, around 8,000 years old. It formed when a mass of gritstone slumped towards the River Dane along a faultline. The resulting void is over 100 metres long and up to 18 metres deep — but, strikingly, just a few metres wide. Both Lud's Church and Castle Rock are composed of Roaches Grit, a harder form of Millstone Grit named after the climber's paradise a mile or so to the south.

40 ♦ TOP 10 WALKS PEAK DISTRICT: Mysterious Walks

Steps, seats and grottoes have been cut into Rowtor Rocks

walk 7

Rowtor Rocks & Cratcliff

Druidic follies, a medieval anchorite's cell and natural gritstone landmarks

What to expect:
Fairly hilly walk between rocky tors, visiting two villages

Distance/time: 6.5 kilometres/4 miles. Allow 2½ hours

Start: Druid Inn in Birchover, DE4 2BL. Street parking nearby

Grid Ref: SK 236 621

Ordnance Survey map: OL24 The Peak District *(White Peak Area)*

After the Walk: Druid Inn, Main Street, Birchover, Matlock DE4 2BL | www.druidbirchover.co.uk | 01629 650424

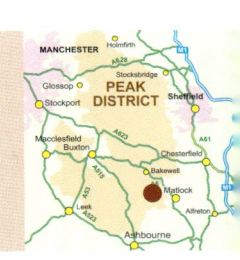

Walk outline

This hilly walk crosses three valleys between gritstone heights in an area rich in curiosities. After an optional clamber around the grottos and other follies of Rowtor Rocks, the walk descends to the B5056 then climbs to the hermitage at Cratcliff Rocks and nearby Robin Hood's Stride. We drop down again into another minor valley before ascending to Elton village, then cross the final valley that divides Elton and Birchover.

Rowtor Rocks, Cratcliff Hermitage & Robin Hood's Stride

Rowtor Rocks were 'enhanced' by Thomas Eyre, an 18th-century clergyman and Druid enthusiast who carved rock rooms, seats, steps and pillars into the gritstone. As a result, some cup-and-ring-marked boulders hereabouts attract a degree of scepticism, though they may be genuinely prehistoric.

No such doubt attaches to the crucifixion carved in the hermit's cave on Cratcliff Crag, a true medieval survival. Nearby Robin Hood's Stride looks at first glance man-made (hence its alternative name of Mock Beggar's Mansion), but its water-worn pinnacles are actually natural.

Druid Inn

Jackdaw

The Walk

1. From the main street in **Birchover**, take the no-through road below the **Druid Inn**. Concessionary access to **Rowtor Rocks** is via a gap at the end of the wall below the pub. Beware of slippery steps and unfenced drops.

2. Returning to the track, follow it down past the **church** to a junction of driveways at the end of the Rowtor Rocks outcrop. Take the track ahead, passing below a garden pond on the left. When the driveway swings sharp left, continue ahead along a track, shortly ignoring a footpath on the right. Keep left at a fork to a stone stile by a gateway and continue past a **part-ruined barn**.

3. Shortly afterwards, turn right off the track through a hand-gate and descend through a scrubby field to the **B5056**. Turn left along the road, past an old milestone on the right.

4. Turn right at a road junction over the stream, then turn immediately right at a **Limestone Way** fingerpost over a cattle grid. Follow the grass-centred private drive. When the drive swings right to **Cratcliff Cottage**, carry on straight up the edge of the field ahead towards Robin Hood's Stride.

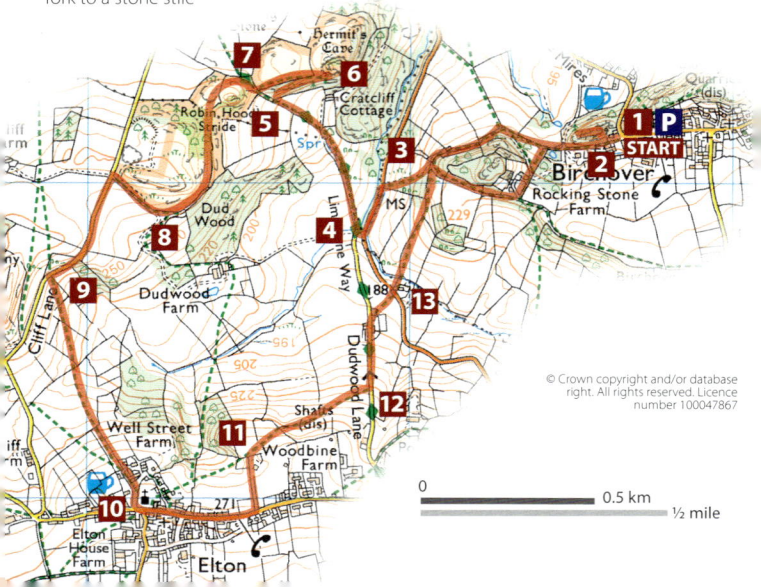

© Crown copyright and/or database right. All rights reserved. Licence number 100047867

Walk 7 – **Rowtor Rocks** & **Cratcliff** ♦ 43

This overhang is one of the many odd features cut into Rowtor Rocks

5. Towards the top of the field, cross to a gate near a bench on the right-hand side which gives access to a concessionary path. Bear right along the wooded slope to a gap in the fence at the end of **Cratcliff Rocks**. Keeping right of most of the boulders, follow a narrow path to view the **hermit's cave**, then return to the same point.

6. This time, take the right-hand stile, . Walk along the top of the wood, then bear right down to a gate in the far right-hand corner. Look right, over the fields, to pick out the four remaining stones of **Nine Stones Close**.

7. Cross a stile opposite the gate and follow the wall to the right of Robin Hood's Stride then pass between scattered trees. Ignoring a path into fields off to the right, pass further **rock outcrops** to reach the edge of a wood. Ignoring a stile in the corner, turn left along a wall with the woodland on your right. Beyond a stone gateway, turn right over a stile by a gate and follow a track along the bottom of a slope on the right.

8. A gate leads to a **small barn**; turn right here and follow the walled track out past a gate to a road. Turn left here and walk downhill.

The strange, ragged rocks of Robin Hood's Stride

9. After 400 metres, a footpath crosses at a left-hand bend; turn left through a gate and walk down through a series of dry-stone walls to the bottom of a small valley. Climb up the other side to a **stone squeeze stile** and continue uphill along the field edge. At the top, turn left into a farm track and follow it round to the right to the rear of **Elton church**.

10. Walk past the church to the **Duke of York pub** and turn left, passing the **primary school** on the left. After the junctions with **Ivy Lane**, **Stone Foot** and **Back Lane** on the right, turn left down a concessionary track to the left of the **cricket pitch**.

11. Beyond the pavilion, climb a stile onto a footpath and bear right. The path descends to a gap, and continues with an overgrown hedge on the left, before crossing a field to **Dudwood Lane**.

12. Turn left. Just beyond **Meadowside**, a stone house with a 1737 datestone, turn right into the driveway and take a footpath beyond a gate in the wall that leads across a field to the **B5056**.

13. Take the path opposite and cross the **stepping stones** at the bottom. At the top of the next field, go through a gate by a stone barn into an enclosed path. At the top of the rise, turn sharp right to a

Walk 7 – **Rowtor Rocks** & **Cratcliff** ♦ 45

gate. Continue past a **ruined barn** whose upper gable is a natural boulder.

14. Pass **Rocking Stone Cottage**, then turn left to pass in front of the property. As the drive curves left, cut across a grassy area on the right to another track. Turn right and retrace your steps to the **Druid Inn** to complete the walk. ♦

Anchorite's Cell

Anchorites led solitary lives of pious contemplation in cells built into churches or natural caves, supported by alms from local donors. The tradition largely ended with the Dissolution, but there is evidence of Haddon Hall providing rabbits to the Cratcliff hermit as late as 1550. Holes and grooves in the cliff imply an external building, probably living quarters, with a chapel in the cave, whose niches and crucifix date from the 13th or 14th century.

TOP 10 WALKS **PEAK DISTRICT: Mysterious Walks**

Two figures emphasise the sheer size of Thor's Cave

walk 8

Thor's Cave

Two dramatic caves overlooking the capricious River Manifold

What to expect:
Dramatic cave visit with a steep descent, rocky spots and a longish climb

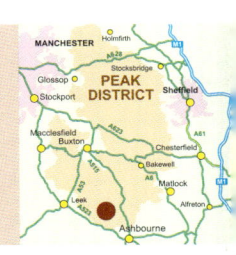

Distance/time: 6.5 kilometres/4 miles. Allow 2–3 hours

Start: Wetton car park, Carr Lane, Wetton DE6 2AF. Overflow parking is sometimes provided in a nearby farmer's field

Grid Ref: SK 109 551

Ordnance Survey map: OL24 The Peak District *(White Peak Area)*

After the Walk: The Royal Oak, Wetton DE6 2AF | www.royaloakwetton.co.uk | 01335310287

Walk outline

A straightforward track leads from Wetton to Thor's Cave. A steep descent via steps and stony ground leads through woodland to a footbridge over the Manifold (usually dry here). There follows an easy stage along an old railway line, to the café at Wetton Mill, where a second cave can be visited. The return is via a typical dry Derbyshire dale and a long, gradual ascent through sheep pastures back to Wetton village.

Thor's Cave and Nan Tor

The huge oval entrance of Thor's Cave overlooks the Manifold valley. Daylight pouring through its two openings mean that the vaulted interior can be explored without artificial lights, though care is needed on the polished limestone.

The quieter Nan Tor Cave, just off the footpath behind the Wetton Mill tearoom, is sometimes cited as an alternative to Lud's Church (see Walk 6) as the location of the 'Green Church', the scene of Sir Gawain and the Green Knight's legendary meeting described in an anonymous medieval poem.

Entrance to Thor's Cave

Greater horseshoe bat

48 ♦ TOP 10 WALKS **PEAK DISTRICT: Mysterious Walks**

The Walk

1. From the **Wetton car park**, turn right past a stone barn in the field on the left, and then right again into a walled lane signposted to 'Wetton Mill'. Pass between two farms, then turn left at the next junction. After 50 metres, take a signposted concessionary track on the left. After 600 metres, beyond a gate and stile, turn right by a 'Wetton' fingerpost into the field on your right.

2. Bear left down the field, passing a wall corner and continue on an obvious, well-worn path across the hillside towards the cave. After a hand-gate, bear right (not towards the top of the hill) onto a path that curves under the cliff to the entrance to **Thor's Cave**.

3. Having explored the cave, take the stepped path in front of the main

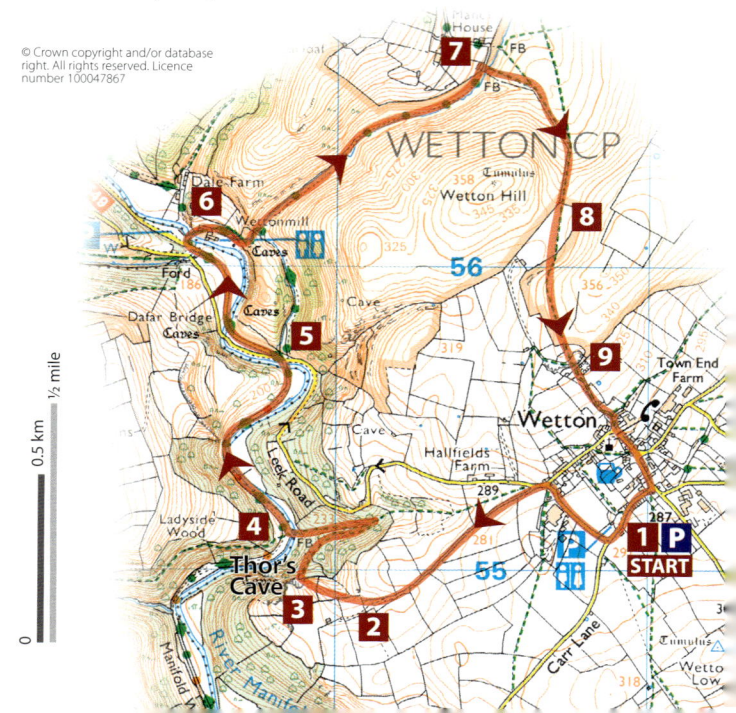

© Crown copyright and/or database right. All rights reserved. Licence number 100047867

Walk 8 – **Thor's Cave** ♦ 49

Nan Tor Cave is reached by a path above Wetton Mill

entrance that winds down through the wood. In the interests of erosion control, ignore any short-cuts on the left until you reach a major crossing path at the bottom of the side-valley, where you turn left (downhill). Follow the path down to the **footbridge** over the (normally dry) **River Manifold** and join the **Manifold Way**, a surfaced cycle and footpath, beyond.

The River Manifold passes under the old packhorse bridge at Wetton Mill as a sparkling limestone stream, but normally disappears into its limestone bed a short distance downstream. The dry riverbed runs below Thor's Cave and the waters only reappear near Ilam, several miles downstream.

4. Turn right and follow the Manifold Way along the valley bottom for half a mile until you cross the river again and meet a public road.

5. Turn left and take the right-hand fork, with a 'Weak Bridge' sign. Cross the dry riverbed once more and continue to the junction at **Wetton Mill**. Turn right over the **old bridge** and bear right to walk in front of the **café**.

The Manifold Valley seen through the main entrance and 'West Window'

6. Follow a signposted footpath between the **farmhouse** (left) and **former stables** (right) up to a gate and into a field. To visit **Nan Tor Cave**, turn immediately left, returning the same way.

Nan Tor Cave is sometimes suggested as an alternative setting for the Green Church, where Sir Gawain confronted the Green Knight. Although Lud's Church is the better-known candidate, in some ways Nan Tor, with its tree-hung interior open to the sky, seems to fit the description in the medieval account rather better.

Continuing along the public footpath, climb the rocky path through a shrubby area, then bear left when it opens out and descend via a hand-gate to the bottom of the unnamed dale. Turn left and follow the path up the dale bottom until you pass a **small swallet** on the right and reach a gate into a metalled road.

7. In front of the **farmhouse**, turn right through a tight **squeeze stile** and cross the stream via a **clapper bridge**. Follow the footpath up the slope and then follow the wall on your right as it climbs through sheep pastures between two hills.

8. Towards the top, cross a stile in the fence (ignoring a wall stile on your right) and leave the wall to follow a path across the field to another stile. The rocky path beyond climbs then levels off across the

Walk 8 – **Thor's Cave** ♦ 51

grassy hillside to a gate and **squeeze stile**, before descending through an **old quarry** to a farm track.

9. Follow the track ahead down into **Wetton village**; bear left past the **Manor House** and pass the **Royal Oak** on your right. At the next road junction, turn right (signposted to Grindon) back to the car park to complete the walk. ♦

Limestone lair

Thor's Cave holds little mystery for 'proper' cavers, having no significant passages beyond the enormous entrance chamber, but has fascinated visitors for centuries, and attracts rock climbers. Nineteenth and early 20th-century excavations found evidence of human occupation since the Stone Age, including at least seven human burials. The dramatic cave featured in Ken Russell's 1988 horror film The Lair of the White Worm, *starring a youthful Hugh Grant.*

52 ♦ TOP 10 WALKS **PEAK DISTRICT: Mysterious Walks**

Strange shrouded tombs in Fenny Bentley church

walk 9

Thorpe & Fenny Bentley

Ecclesiastical curiosities and the remains of a fortified manor house

What to expect:
Fairly hilly, farmland walk between two villages

Distance/time: 5.5 kilometres/3½ miles. Allow 2 hours

Start: Narlow Lane car park, Thorpe DE4 2BL

Grid Ref: SK 011 892

Ordnance Survey map: OL24 The Peak District *(White Peak Area)*

After the Walk: The Coach and Horses, Fenny Bentley DE6 1LB | 01335 350246

Walk outline

This hilly walk turns its back on the attractions of Dovedale to explore two intriguing villages to the east. From a high starting point we descend to Wash Brook, then climb the intervening ridge to Fenny Bentley in the next valley. The sequence is reversed on the return, followed by a stretch of the Tissington Trail before crossing a third and final valley below Thorpe.

Thor's Cave and Nan Tor

Thorpe church has a squat Norman tower with round-headed bell-openings typical of the era. An 18th-century sundial in the churchyard is too tall to be read comfortably from normal eye level — the mystery is solved when one realises that it was designed to be consulted from horseback.

The church at Fenny Bentley looks unremarkable from the outside, but has a couple of curiosities within: a carved wooden screen from the early 1500s and the unsettling Beresford tombs. The Beresfords lived at nearby Bentley Hall, which retains its square medieval tower.

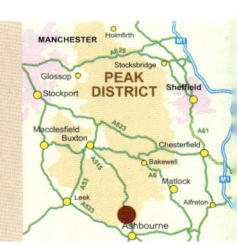

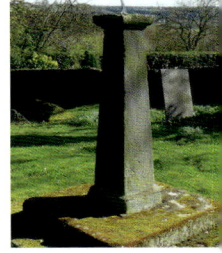

Sundial, Thorpe churchyard

Wild arum

The Walk

1. From the **car park**, walk down **Narlow Lane** away from the **Old Dog pub**. At a junction on a bend, bear right at a parking sign. Before a house on the right, take a footpath on the left that runs parallel to the road then passes under the **Tissington Trail**. Continue ahead down to a **footbridge** over the **Wash Brook**.

2. Bear right to a gate and continue in a similar direction diagonally up the field beyond to a gate in the top right-hand corner. Follow the right-hand edge of a sheep field to a double hand-gate in a hedge and proceed down the centre of the next field, eventually meeting a hedge on the left and passing a bungalow. Go through a gate by a farm building and walk down to a metalled lane. Turn left and walk down through **Fenny Bentley village**.

3. Turn right into the **churchyard** and walk past the **church** to the **lychgate**, which gives access to the main **A515 road**. Cross carefully and turn right, passing **Cherry Orchard Farm** and the **Coach and Horses pub** on your left.

With the possible exception of the font and south doorway, nothing remains of the original Norman church at Fenny Bentley. The existing building dates mainly from

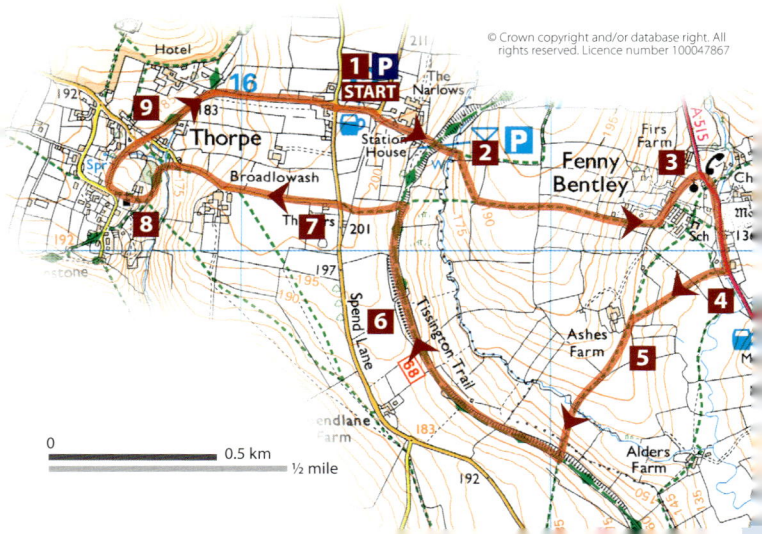

Bentley Hall features a medieval square defensive tower

the 14th century, though it was heavily restored between 1847 and 1850, and a spire added in 1864. Nearby Cherry Orchard Farm, formerly known as Bentley Hall and home to the Beresfords, is a Grade II* listed building and consists of a late medieval buttressed tower attached to a 17th-century farmhouse, which was modified in the late 19th century. The tower has sometimes been interpreted as a gatehouse for a lost hall that stood within a moat.

4. Beyond the pub, at **Rose Cottage**, cross the main road again and follow a footpath over the **Bentley Brook** via a **slab bridge** and past a house to a gate into fields. Bear slightly left and pass to the left of a fenced-off area, then continue to a hand-gate in a hedge next to a field gate. Climb to another hand-gate in a wooden fence below **Ashes Farm**.

5. Cross the field past a waymark post (with the farm to your right) to a gate in the field corner, beyond which cross a farm track and follow the hedge steeply down to a **footbridge** over **Wash Brook**. Climb the steep valley side beyond to the **Tissington Trail**, where you turn right.

St Leonard's Church in Thorpe has typically Norman round-headed arches

The Tissington Trail follows the line of the former Ashbourne to Buxton railway, part of the London and North Western Railway, which opened in 1899 and closed in 1967.

6. After half a mile, pass under a high **overbridge**. Continue for 300 metres to a crossing path, where you leave the Trail, turning left (signposted 'Public Footpath to Thorpe') through a kissing gate. Climb the field beyond to a gate in a hedge and follow a fence out to the road. For a quick return to the start, turn right here, but to visit **Thorpe village** (recommended), cross over into the lane to **The Firs**, opposite.

7. Beyond the house continue along the lane to a farm, with views to Thorpe Cloud. Shortly after the **farm**, climb a stile on the left into a field and bear right with the lane on your right, heading down to a stile and **footbridge** at the valley bottom. Turn left along a path with a wall to the left that climbs the opposite side of the valley.

8. Below the **church**, turn right, then go left through a gate into the **churchyard**. Exit beyond the church building and bear right past a couple of benches. Turn right by the **village hall** down a narrow lane (**Hall Lane**) to a road junction.

9. Turn right and follow the road past **Thorpe Cottage** (ignoring the turning on the right). Climb the hill past the **Peveril of the Peak hotel** back to the **Old Dog** to complete the walk.

An unexpected curiosity near the Old Dog is 'Pipes in the Peaks' — a restored Compton organ purchased from a Derby cinema and installed in the rather incongruous surroundings of a car repair shop and garage. ♦

Shrouded tombs

The Beresford tombs in Fenny Bentley church show Thomas Beresford (died 1473) and his wife anonymously bundled in pleated shrouds. Around the sides of the tomb their children are also depicted in shrouds, described by architectural historian Nikolaus Pevsner as 'a weird, grotesque idea'. The pragmatic explanation for this creepy design decision is that the tombs were carved long after the deaths of the occupants and no likeness survived to guide the sculptor.

58 ♦ TOP 10 WALKS **PEAK DISTRICT: Mysterious Walks**

Halter Devil Chapel sits at the heart of a local legend

walk 10

Halter Devil Chapel

The story of a terrifying night-time encounter and a repentant farmer

What to expect:
Rolling farmland, with mud possible after rain; one steep bank and numerous stiles

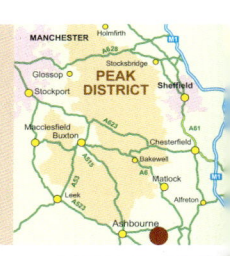

Distance/time: 7.5 kilometres/4½ miles. Allow 2–3 hours

Start: Cock Inn, Mugginton, or roadside parking to north; DE6 4PJ

Grid Ref: SK 287 440

Ordnance Survey map: Explorer 259 Derby

After the Walk: The Cock Inn, junction of Bullhurst and Church Lane, Mugginton DE6 4PJ | www.cockinnmugginton.com | 01773550703

Walk outline

The former Ravensdale deer park covers a series of sandy hills divided by valleys, so there are some moderate ascents and descents. Beyond Halter Devil Chapel we cross a stream and head below sand quarries to Mercaston Marsh and Mugginton Bottoms (an SSSI), followed by a pleasant bridleway to Mugginton, from where a gentle climb through the village leads back to the start.

Mugginton and the Halter Devil Chapel

The main visible remnant of the Ravensdale deer park is the 'park pale' — an earthwork and fence designed to allow deer in, but not out. One side of the central north–south valley is occupied by a belt of narrow fields, still noticeable on a modern map: this was the 'deer course' along which deer were chased by dogs.

Halter Devil is an 18th-century chapel attached to a modest farmhouse. The doorposts of Mugginton church are deeply scored, popularly believed to be by local archers sharpening their arrows. However, expert opinion suggests that these marks are where dust was scraped from holy buildings for use in folk remedies.

Archery or medicine?

Common lousewort

The Walk

1. Behind the **Cock Inn**, cross **Church Lane** and follow a track to the right of a house to a bungalow at the edge of a wood; follow the drive right then take a path left of the entrance, dropping through trees to a stile into fields. Bear half-right to another stile beside a gate. Follow the hedge to **Old Covert Farm**.

Cross the drive onto a footpath that crosses a stile and climbs to a hand-gate. Descend to **Park Farm**.

2. Turn right through a gate. After 250 metres, leave the driveway, continuing ahead on a tree-lined track. Walk past a house and through a hand-gate into fields. Pass to the right of a tree to **Parkhill Farm**, where a stile gives access to the farmyard. Follow the footpath right, between the buildings, then turn left past the farmhouse.

3. Continue through a gate, along the field edge and between gorse bushes to a pair of gateways. Go through the hand-gate to the left and follow the hedge to another gateway.

© Crown copyright and/or database right. All rights reserved. Licence number 100047867

Walk 10 – **Halter Devil Chapel** ♦ 61

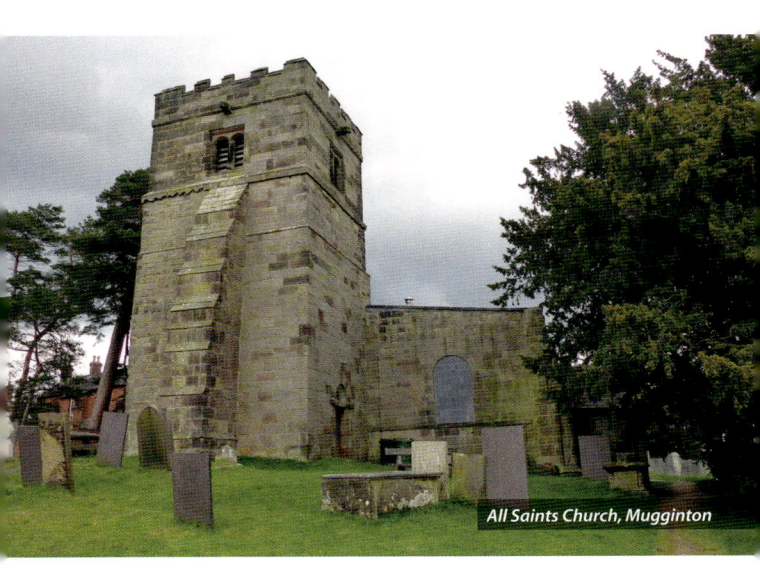

All Saints Church, Mugginton

In the next field, aim towards a **large house** to a **footbridge**. Turn left between **stream** and **pond** and follow a fence to the right across lawns to a driveway. Turn left along another fence and up steps. Leave the fence past a waymark post on the left to the road.

4. Turn left, passing **Blackbrook Farm** and **Halter Devil Chapel.** Just after a triangular junction, take a gate on the left and follow the footpath right, over a stile and a rough field to a drive. Turn left then right, passing a triple garage and through a couple of gates into a track to a further gate. Bear right across paddocks separated by hand-gates to a stream in the right-hand corner.

5. Climb the steep slope beyond, aided by a rope, to a stile. Cross a track and a bridge over a conveyor belt. After a gate, continue parallel to the valley on your right. Descend to a gateway in a dry valley then climb to another gate and follow the hedge beyond. At a gate in the hedge, switch sides and continue uphill along the field boundary. Beyond a gateway, bear left to the top left-hand corner, to a waymarked gate into a track above **Hill Top Farm**.

The curious Halter Devil Chapel adjoins a Georgian farmhouse

6. Cross and go through a metal field gate. Proceed to a hand-gate left of a barn, then head for the far left-hand corner of the next field. Go through a farm gate and follow the track ahead. At the bottom of the slope, turn right through a hand-gate onto a footpath. Follow the field edge to **Schoolhouse Farm**.

7. Follow the drive through the farm and across the valley bottom. At a bend by a **stream**, turn left along a bridleway which shortly fords the stream before continuing between trees to a gate. Follow the bridleway below a series of fields to meet a wider track. Turn right over a stile and walk up the side of a field above a pond, through a **stone squeeze stile** and past a house up to the **church**.

8. Turn left (uphill) through the **village**, passing the **primary school**. Pass The **Old Beeches** and then a bridleway on the left, then turn left up a driveway with a public footpath sign. After a metal gate, bear right to pass to the left of a hedged garden to a hand-gate. Cross to another hand-gate and continue towards **farm buildings** ahead.

9. Keep left of the farm buildings and follow the woodland edge on your left. When you reach the bungalow you passed on your outward journey;

turn right to return to the **Cock Inn** to complete the walk.

Visitors may be surprised to see a horse, rather than a chicken, on the sign for the Cock Inn. In the days of horse-drawn transport, carters bound for Derby would hire an extra horse for the steep pull from Weston Underwood, then leave the borrowed 'cock horse' at the inn. ♦

Halter Devil Chapel
Farmer Francis Brown set out drunkenly one stormy night to fetch some coal. Struggling to harness his skittish horse, he cursed that 'If I can't halter thee, I'll halter the Devil.' Here, versions of the story diverge: either the animal disappeared in a puff of smoke, or a flash of lightning revealed a horned beast. Either way, the farmer was shocked into sobriety and, to make amends, in 1723 built the chapel abutting his farmhouse.

Useful Information

Visit Peak District & Derbyshire
The official tourist website with the latest information on attractions, activities, events, accommodation and eating out: **www.visitpeakdistrict.com**

Peak District National Park
The National Park website gives practical details of tourist information centres, visitor attractions, public transport, car parks and public toilets. **www.peakdistrict.gov.uk**

Visitor Centres
The official National Park authority has four main TIC's offering advice on accommodation, transport and ideas for local attractions and activities:

Bakewell	01629 813227	bakewell@peakdistrict.gov.uk
Castleton	01629 816572	castleton@peakdistrict.gov.uk
Edale	01433 670207	edale@peakdistrict.gov.uk
Upper Derwent	01433 650953	derwentinfo@peakdistrict.gov.uk

Local Museums
Buxton Museum and Art Gallery has permanent collections of fossils, social history, local crafts and fine art. **www.derbyshire.gov.uk/leisure/buxton-museum/buxton-museum-and-art-gallery.aspx** | 01629 533540 | buxton.museum@derbyshire.gov.uk

The Museum of Making in Derby charts the progress of Derby's manufacturing history and the people involved. **www.derbymuseums.org/museum-of-making** | 01332 641901 | info@derbymuseums.org

Public Transport
www.peakdistrict.gov.uk/visiting/planning-your-visit/publictransport provides a useful starting point for planning a visit by train or bus. **www.traveline.info** (0871 200 22 33) has detailed timetable information.

Weather
The Met Office operates a 24-hour online weather forecast for places in Derbyshire and the Peak District: **www.metoffice.gov.uk**

Recommended Reading
Frank Rodgers' *Curiosities of the Peak District* (1979) and *More Curiosities of the Peak District* (2000) are out of print, but full of inspiration for further quirky places to visit.